C000142112

GODDESS ISIS

THE MAGICAL HEALER

Goddess Isis - The Magical Healer

Copyright © Nichole Muir

All right reserved. No part of this book may be reproduced by any mechanical, photographic, or electronic process, or in the form of a phonographic recording: nor may it be stored in a retrieval system, transmitted, or otherwise be copied for public or private use- other than for "fair use" as brief quotation embodied in articles and reviews – without prior written permission of the publisher

Please note the information contained within this document is for educational and entertainment purposes only. All effort has been executed to present accurate, up to date, and reliable, complete information. No warranties of any kind are declared or implied.

Readers acknowledge that the author is not engaging in the rendering of legal, financial, medical or professional advice. The content within this book has been derived from various sources. Please consult a licensed professional before attempting any techniques outlined in this book.

Contents

Chapter 1: The Enigma of Isis

In the golden sands of ancient Egypt, among the magnificent pyramids and timeless temples, thrived a pantheon of deities and gods. Yet, none shone as luminously as Isis—the mother of magic, a beacon of hope, and the epitome of resilience. Isis's story is not just of a deity but of a symbol that has transcended time, influencing various cultures and societies, extending far beyond her Egyptian origins. This chapter aims to unveil the enigma of Isis, leading you through her captivating myths, deciphering the symbolism she embodies, and introducing the archetype of the magical healer.

Origins and Myths

Isis, known as 'Aset' in ancient Egyptian, was considered one of the most significant deities in the Egyptian pantheon. Her origin traces back to the earliest dynastic periods, and over time, her veneration spread across the breadth of the ancient world, from Egypt to Greece and even Rome.

Her myths are woven with threads of magic, compassion, and determination. One of the most poignant tales involves her beloved husband Osiris and the treacherous god Set. Jealous of Osiris' fame and position, Set plotted against him, leading to Osiris' death and dismemberment. Refusing to accept this fate, Isis scoured the land, seeking every fragment of her husband, displaying an unwavering love and devotion. With her magical prowess, she resurrected Osiris long enough for their union to conceive their son, Horus. This myth not only highlights her role as a dedicated wife and loving mother but also underscores her powerful magical abilities.

Another myth tells of Isis obtaining the secret name of Ra, the sun god. By crafting a snake from the earth mixed with Ra's saliva, she orchestrated a scenario where the serpent bit Ra, causing him immense pain. The only cure lay in invoking his secret name, which he reluctantly shared with Isis. This story paints her as a cunning and strategic deity, attributes that would resonate with her worshippers seeking solutions to their earthly problems.

Symbolism Behind the Deity

The imagery and symbols associated with Isis are as diverse as the myths that encompass her. Often, she's depicted as a woman wearing a throne-shaped crown or with outstretched wings, symbolizing her protective nature. The ankh, a symbol of life, is frequently seen in her grasp, reaffirming her role as a giver and restorer of life.

Her role as a mother is not only restricted to her son, Horus. She is the divine mother—nurturer of pharaohs and the common folk alike. In many illustrations, she is seen nursing her son, an emblematic representation of the royal lineage's divine protection and the sustenance she provides to the world.

The knot of Isis, also known as 'tyet', is another symbol intertwined with her persona. It resembles an ankh but with pointed arms. This amulet, often made of red jasper or carnelian, symbolized protection and was believed to carry the magic of Isis, shielding its bearer from harm.

The Archetype of the Magical Healer

Isis is not just a deity to be revered. She embodies the archetype of the magical healer—a figure that resonates across various cultures and timelines. This archetype is not merely about the act of healing physical ailments. It's about a holistic approach to wellness, encompassing the body, mind, and spirit.

Throughout her myths, Isis displays profound knowledge of spells, incantations, and natural remedies. She's both a protector and restorer, attributes essential for a healer. When she sought the fragmented body of Osiris, her journey symbolized the soul's quest for wholeness, a theme prevalent even in modern healing practices.

Her ability to resurrect Osiris epitomizes the idea that healing is not just about curing; it's about rejuvenation and rebirth. In our lives, we often face metaphorical deaths—losses, endings, or significant changes. The archetype of Isis encourages us to piece together the fragments, to seek rebirth and renewal instead of dwelling in despair.

Isis also exemplifies the balance between knowledge and wisdom. While her cunning in obtaining Ra's secret name highlights her strategic nature, it also underscores the importance of seeking knowledge to benefit and heal others. The act wasn't just about empowerment; it was about wielding power responsibly.

Isis's allure lies not just in her tales but in the timeless symbols and archetypes she represents. As we delve deeper into her world, we don't just discover a deity; we uncover aspects of ourselves. The strength in the face of despair, the resilience amidst challenges, and the innate desire to heal and protect are attributes that echo within each of us. Through understanding Isis, we embrace these facets, beginning our journey towards holistic healing and self-discovery.

Chapter 2: Roots of Healing

The tales and scrolls of ancient civilizations have always held within them a deep reverence for the mysteries of the human body, the spirit, and the interplay between them. Of all the ancient civilizations, Egypt stands out not just for its monumental pyramids and iconic hieroglyphs but also for its profound understanding of the health and well-being of both the soul and the body. At the very heart of this ancient Egyptian approach to healing was the venerated goddess, Isis.

Ancient Methods of Healing: The Egyptian Way

The Nile, with its life-sustaining waters, was the lifeblood of ancient Egyptian civilization. Around its fertile banks, a rich tapestry of spiritual and medical practices evolved, deeply intertwined and inseparable. To truly grasp the essence of Egyptian healing, one must understand it as a blend of the physical and the ethereal, the tangible and the mystic.

Egyptian priests and physicians didn't merely focus on treating physical ailments; they perceived illnesses as a disbalance that could be rooted in spiritual, emotional, or environmental causes. Consequently, the Egyptian medical toolkit comprised not just herbs and surgeries, but also incantations, charms, and rituals.

Papyrus scrolls, some of the earliest known medical texts, offer a window into the treatments and beliefs of the time. One such document, the Ebers Papyrus, details over 700 remedies for various ailments, from simple garlic concoctions for heart problems to incantations meant to ward off evil spirits causing illness.

Another crucial aspect of ancient Egyptian medicine was the concept of Ma'at, which

Introduction to Egyptian Magic

Egyptian magic, or heka, was seen as a divine force given by the gods to humans, allowing them to ward off the ill-intentions of enemies, cure illnesses, and guarantee safe passage into the afterlife. More than mere sorcery or illusion, heka was a deeply spiritual practice intertwined with religion, medicine, and astrology.

To the Egyptians, the universe operated on ma'at, an abstract yet central concept that represented order, balance, and truth. Magic was a tool to maintain or restore this balance. If chaos ever threatened to disrupt this harmony, rituals and spells were performed to appease the gods and realign with the forces of ma'at.

Tools, Symbols, and Rituals: Tapping into the Magic

Various tools were crucial for the practice of Egyptian magic. Among them, the most significant were:

The Ankh: Known as the key of life, the ankh symbolized both mortal existence and the afterlife. Priests and magicians often held it during rituals, believing it channeled the power of life and immortality.

The Djed Pillar: Resembling a column with four horizontal lines, it was seen as the backbone of the god Osiris. It became synonymous with stability, regeneration, and the enduring strength of the gods.

The Was Scepter: A long staff, often with the head of a canine deity at its top, symbolized power and dominion. It was believed to grant authority to the one who wielded it, often seen in depictions of gods and pharaohs.

Magic also thrived through symbols like hieroglyphs. These sacred inscriptions were more than mere writing; they carried with them profound energy. When inscribed on tombs or scrolls, they could invoke protection, prosperity, and blessings.

The potency of Egyptian magic was further magnified by rituals. Rituals bridged the gap between the mortal realm and the divine, creating a conduit for energies to flow. One such ritual was the "Opening of the Mouth" ceremony, ensuring that the deceased could speak and eat in the afterlife. Another vital ritual was the daily temple ritual, where statues of gods were cleansed, clothed, and offered food. This ritual ensured the deity's favor and blessings upon the land.

Isis' Magical Teachings

In the pantheon of Egyptian deities, Isis stood out as the embodiment of magic. Often depicted with wings and an ankh, she was revered as the goddess of healing, protection, and rebirth. Her magical prowess was legendary, transcending the boundaries of life and death.

The tales of her resurrecting her husband Osiris from the dead are not just stories of undying love but also testimonies to her unparalleled magical abilities. She pieced him back together after his brother Set had dismembered him, showcasing her deep knowledge of life forces and rebirth.

Isis's magic was intrinsically tied to her role as a mother and protector. She fiercely protected her son, Horus, from the treachery of Set, using her magic to heal and shield him. This story reinforces her unwavering commitment to healing and safeguarding those she loved.

One of Isis' most profound teachings was the understanding of true names. In Egyptian belief, knowing the true name of a being or object meant having dominion over it. Isis once cunningly acquired the true name of the sun god Ra, which gave her immense power. This tale underscores the importance of knowledge, words, and the act of naming in magic.

Her teachings extended to everyday Egyptians. Through prayers, amulets, and spells dedicated to her, she granted protection during childbirth, cured illnesses, and offered solace to those in distress. Her magic wasn't just for grand, mythical tales—it touched the lives of all who invoked her.

Egyptian magic, with its intricate rituals, powerful symbols, and divine invocations, offers a glimpse into a world where the boundaries between the natural and supernatural were fluid. The magic within was a force recognized, revered, and integrated into daily life. Isis, with her profound magical teachings, stood as a beacon, illuminating the path for all seekers of wisdom, healing, and protection. Through her, we understand that magic is not just about wielding power, but about understanding the deeper harmonies of existence and our place within the vast cosmos.

Chapter 4: Embracing the Maternal Spirit

The core of ancient Egyptian mythology is replete with gods and goddesses, each representing facets of human emotion, nature, and experience. Yet, amongst this pantheon, few deities resonate with the depths of emotion, protection, and love as powerfully as Isis. As the embodiment of the maternal spirit, her presence illuminates how maternal energy can be a potent source of deep healing and rejuvenation.

Isis as the Mother Goddess: Symbols and Significance

Isis, whose name might be translated to "Throne" in the ancient Egyptian language, is not merely a goddess. She epitomizes the maternal archetype, often portrayed with a throne-like hieroglyphic emblem on her head, symbolizing her as the seat of pharaonic power. But more than just a representation of royalty, this symbolism alludes to her foundational role in the lives of both gods and humans. She is the cornerstone upon which the constructs of nurturance, protection, and sustenance are built.

The myths surrounding Isis further amplify her maternal aspects. In the story of Osiris's death, her husband and brother, it is Isis's unwavering love and determination that brings him back to life. She searches tirelessly for his scattered remains, protects their son Horus from the wrath of Set, and even harnesses her magical abilities to resurrect Osiris, albeit temporarily. This tale, amongst many others, positions Isis not just as a mother but as the epitome of maternal devotion and resilience.

The ankh, a symbol often associated with Isis, stands for life. As a mother goddess, Isis wields the ankh, bestowing life, ensuring the flow of the Nile, and maintaining the balance between life and death. Her wings, often depicted spread in protection or wrapped around her loved ones, are emblematic of her role as a guardian, always ready to shield and safeguard.

How Maternal Energy Can Be a Source of Deep Healing

Maternal energy transcends the physical act of giving birth. It encompasses a broad spectrum of emotions and actions — from the gentleness of a lullaby to the fierce protectiveness in the face of danger. This energy, deeply woven into the fabric of Isis's narrative, holds profound healing properties.

Imagine the kind of unwavering love that drives a deity to piece back her murdered husband or protect her child against all odds. This is the depth and breadth of maternal love. It is a love that heals wounds, bridges gaps, and, in many ways, defies logic. Embracing such love in our lives, whether by channeling it or receiving it, can be a significant source of healing. It reminds us of our worth, our significance, and our inherent right to wholeness.

When we think of healing, our minds often jump to the physical — the mending of a broken bone or the subsiding of an illness. But the most profound wounds are often intangible: the scars of betrayal, the pain of loss, the ache of longing. Here, maternal energy, with its inherent tenderness and strength, becomes the salve. It does not just cover the wound; it goes to its very root, addressing, comforting, and restoring.

Connecting with Your Own Maternal Instincts

Regardless of gender, age, or whether one has borne a child, the maternal instinct is an intrinsic part of our psyche. This instinct isn't just about procreation; it's about creation, protection, and nurturing in all its forms.

To connect with this instinct is to understand one's capacity for profound love and the potential for healing oneself and others. Begin by tapping into memories of maternal figures in your life — be it your mother, a guardian, or even a teacher. Remember moments of sheer, unconditional love. Let these memories wash over you, reminding you of your own capability to love, protect, and heal.

Meditation is a potent tool in this journey. Picture yourself in the embrace of Isis, feel her wings wrapped around you, her strength becoming yours. As you breathe, internalize her energy, allowing it to reawaken the maternal spirit within you. Remember, this isn't about becoming a mother in the literal sense. It's about embodying the qualities associated with it: compassion, resilience, and unconditional love.

Another approach is to nurture — whether it's taking care of a plant, adopting a pet, or simply caring for a loved one. The act of nurturing hones the maternal instinct, making one more attuned to the ebbs and flows of this potent energy.

The maternal spirit, as exemplified by Isis, is an ageless and powerful source of healing. To embrace it is to open oneself to deeper connections, profound healing, and the infinite magic of unconditional love. Whether you're invoking the energy of Isis or tapping into your reservoir of maternal instincts, remember that this journey is about honoring the nurturing essence that resides within us all.

Chapter 5: The Art of Resilience

Resilience, often envisioned as the ability to bounce back from adversities and maintain mental and emotional fortitude, is not a modern concept. Ancient tales, epics, and myths have shown how resilience was always integral to the human spirit. Among these tales, the stories of Isis, the revered Egyptian goddess, stand out as compelling chronicles of strength, endurance, and undying perseverance.

Stories of Isis' Strength and Endurance

The story of Isis is imbued with elements of love, betrayal, magic, and, most importantly, resilience. She is often depicted with wings spread wide, symbolizing protection, and her legendary tales resonate deeply with themes of restoration and regeneration.

One of the most poignant episodes is the tale of her husband Osiris's death at the hands of his brother Set. Driven by jealousy and ambition, Set plotted against Osiris, ending up dismembering his body and scattering the parts throughout Egypt. The grief of losing her beloved was immense for Isis, but she did not let despair take her. With unwavering determination, she began her quest to search for every part of Osiris.

Accompanied by her sister Nephthys, Isis roamed the lands, faced numerous challenges, and collected each of Osiris's parts. With her potent magic and deep love, she managed to resurrect him, showcasing an unparalleled example of resilience. This story, while highlighting the trials and tribulations of Isis, serves as a testament to her indomitable spirit.

Another manifestation of Isis's strength was her role in conceiving and protecting her son, Horus. Aware of Set's malice and knowing that he would attempt to harm her offspring, Isis took refuge among the reeds of the Nile Delta, hiding and nurturing her son in seclusion. This narrative exemplifies her role as a protective mother, willing to face any danger to safeguard her child. The tales of her battles against Set to protect her son further emphasize her relentless resolve.

Building Your Inner Strength: Lessons from the Goddess

Drawing parallels between the divine stories of Isis and our mortal existence, there are several lessons one can derive from her tales of strength.

Faith in Love: Isis's quest to recover Osiris's body wasn't solely based on her magical powers; it was her unwavering love and faith in it that gave her strength. In life, when faced with adversity, remembering the love we have – be it for family, friends, or a passion – can guide and bolster our spirits.

Embrace Change and Uncertainty: Just as Isis had to adapt to new circumstances, be it the death of Osiris or the birth and protection of Horus in hiding, we must learn to accept and navigate the unpredictable tides of life. By embracing change, we unlock an inherent flexibility, allowing us to approach challenges with grace.

Perseverance is Key: In every story about Isis, one thing remains constant - her perseverance. Whether it was searching for Osiris's body or protecting her son from Set, she never gave up. This lesson is paramount. In our quests, no matter how insurmountable the challenges seem, consistent effort and an unyielding spirit often lead to rewards.

The Connection Between Resilience and Healing

Isis's narratives are not just about showcasing her resilience; they also emphasize the theme of healing. When she reconstructed Osiris, it was an act of physical and emotional healing. When she protected Horus, she was preserving the future, ensuring healing for generations to come.

Resilience and healing are intrinsically linked. Resilience is not just the capacity to bounce back but also to grow and heal through the adversities. The process of facing challenges head-on, much like Isis did, leads to a form of internal healing. As we navigate life's challenges, our resilience helps us recover, regenerate, and rebuild, akin to the phoenix rising from its ashes.

Healing is not merely the absence of pain or distress; it's the growth and wisdom garnered from those experiences. As with Isis, her trials, though painful, led her to become one of the most powerful and revered deities in the Egyptian pantheon. Her resilience was her path to healing.

In our lives, as we face adversities, we must remember that with resilience comes profound healing. Every challenge offers a lesson, and every setback can be a setup for a comeback. The tales of Isis remind us that with unwavering spirit and determination, not only can we overcome challenges, but we can also transform and heal in ways we never deemed possible.

In concluding this chapter, one must introspect and ask, "How can I embody the resilience of Isis in my life?" The answer lies within, in our strengths, our love, our perseverance, and our capacity to heal. By embracing these, we not only honor the tales of the great goddess but also chart a path of profound growth and healing for ourselves.

Chapter 6: Lighting the Flame of Hope

In the shimmering annals of history, hope has always emerged as a powerful and intangible force that binds the human spirit, driving us to persevere and flourish even amidst adversity. Ancient Egypt, with its vast and intricate belief system, revered hope as an essential element of existence, intricately weaving it into their myths, rituals, and daily practices.

Hope in Ancient Egyptian Beliefs

Egyptians viewed life as a cycle, similar to the Nile's rhythmic ebbing and flowing, which nurtured their lands and souls alike. Hope, for them, wasn't merely a fleeting sentiment but an integral part of their cosmology. The Nile's annual inundation represented rebirth, rejuvenation, and, naturally, hope. After all, a land that could be renewed annually by the river's floodwaters spoke of nature's ability to resurrect, renew, and restore.

Furthermore, the very architecture of Egypt speaks volumes about their philosophy on hope. The pyramids, massive and enduring, are testimonials to the Egyptians' belief in the continuity of life beyond death, and the eternal journey of the soul. Hope was not constrained to the temporal world but spanned the realms of life, death, and rebirth.

The Guiding Light of Isis

At the center of this intricate web of beliefs stood Isis, the goddess of healing, magic, and motherhood. Isis, in her multifaceted roles, was also the torchbearer of hope. The tales of her relentless quest to find the fragments of her slain husband, Osiris, showcase her indomitable spirit and unwavering hope. This narrative, among others, offered solace to the bereaved, suggesting that death wasn't the end but a mere transition.

Isis's role as the mother of Horus, the god of the sky and kingship, further amplifies her connection to hope. Her meticulous care in nurturing and protecting Horus from the wrath of Set, the god of chaos and disorder, served as a divine exemplification of a mother's hope for her child's bright future.

Beyond mythology, Isis was a beacon of hope in daily life. Her temples were places of solace and healing. The sick and the wounded, both in spirit and body, would seek her blessings, drawing strength from her tales and her statues, often depicted with widespread wings, sheltering the Pharaohs or her believers, suggesting protection and the promise of better days.

Techniques to Cultivate and Maintain Hope in Modern Times

The ancient Egyptians, with their profound reverence for life's cyclical nature, can teach us a great deal about fostering hope in today's ever-changing world.

Nature's Rhythms: Just as the Egyptians respected the Nile's patterns, we can draw hope from nature's rhythms around us. Seasons change, reminding us of life's transient nature, and with every winter's end, spring arrives, representing new beginnings. By staying attuned to these natural cycles, we can internalize the belief that after every dark phase, there will be light.

Narratives of Resilience: Isis's tales of overcoming challenges can be reflected upon in moments of despair. Dive deep into mythologies, not just Egyptian, but from various cultures. Such stories can serve as metaphoric reservoirs of hope, reminding us of the human spirit's strength and resilience.

Daily Acts of Hope: Engage in small daily rituals that represent hope for you. It could be as simple as lighting a candle every evening, symbolizing the conquest of light over darkness, or tending to a plant, nurturing its growth and reflecting on your own journey.

Community and Connection: The temples of Isis were centers of community gatherings. In modern times, building and staying connected with a community – be it a group of like-minded individuals, support groups, or even virtual communities – can act as a stronghold of collective hope. Sharing stories, experiences, and aspirations can reinforce belief in better tomorrows.

Mindfulness and Meditation: Channel the teachings of Isis through mindful practices. Meditation can ground us, helping in clearing the mental clutter and reconnecting with our inner reservoirs of hope. Techniques that focus on breath, visualization, or even guided meditations centered around the imagery of Isis can be particularly effective.

Hope Journals: Maintain a diary dedicated to hope. Document moments that instilled hope in you, list down quotes, anecdotes, or even dreams that echo hope's sentiment. In moments of despair, this journal can serve as a reminder of the countless times hope has steered you forward.

Seek Inspiration: From art to literature, immerse yourself in works that echo hope's ethos. Let music, paintings, poems, and narratives infuse your spirit with hope, reminding you of its timeless and universal nature.

Hope, as exemplified by the ancient Egyptians and their reverence for Isis, is neither a passive sentiment nor a fleeting emotion. It's an active practice, a daily commitment to believing in the unseen, the unmanifested. In today's world, where uncertainties loom large, the lessons from the sands of Egypt and the guiding light of Isis can illuminate our path, ensuring that the flame of hope, once lit, never falters.

Chapter 7: The Sanctuary of Silence: Introduction to Meditation

Throughout the annals of history, countless civilizations have cultivated practices that seek inner peace and connection with the divine. Ancient Egypt, with its grand pyramids and mysterious deities, was no exception. Their civilization was deeply spiritual, rooted in a profound understanding of the cosmos, nature, and the human psyche. Meditation, though not in the form we typically conceive of it today, played a significant role in their spiritual repertoire. It acted as a bridge, allowing them to connect with the divine energies and discover their inner sanctuaries.

The Role of Meditation in Ancient Egyptian Practices

To comprehend the place of meditation in ancient Egyptian traditions, one must first understand their worldview. The Egyptians perceived life as an intertwined dance of the physical and the metaphysical. For them, the spiritual realm was as palpable as the shifting sands of their desert landscapes. The temples, pyramids, and sacred sites were not just stone structures but physical manifestations of their profound spiritual beliefs. These were places where the veil between the earthly and divine realms was thin, where priests, priestesses, and initiates could access higher realms.

Historical texts and murals depict priests and other high-ranking individuals in meditative postures, often surrounded by symbols representing various gods and cosmic elements. These were not just artistic representations but intricate records of the spiritual rituals of the time.

While the exact methodologies might remain shrouded in mystery, it's evident that the act of focused contemplation, ritual chants, and attunement to divine energies were central to their practice. This was their form of meditation— a deep, inner journey to connect with divine forces and, in particular, deities like Isis.

Discovering Your Inner Temple

Much like the ancient Egyptians, each of us carries an 'inner temple'— a sanctuary within where we can retreat from the external world and connect with our true essence. This sacred space is not bound by the confines of physical walls but is expansive, echoing the vastness of the universe. It is a place of immense peace, wisdom, and energy.

Accessing this inner temple requires silencing the external noises and distractions. It demands that we shed our earthly concerns and let go of the chaos that often clouds our mind. As we quieten the mind, we begin to perceive the whispers of our soul, the subtle energies that dance within and around us.

For the Egyptians, the inner temple was where they communed with the gods. It was the sanctum where divine guidance, wisdom, and energy flowed. By discovering and frequently visiting our inner temple through meditation, we can access the same timeless wisdom and insight that guided ancient civilizations.

Beginning Your Meditation Journey with the Guidance of Isis

For those new to meditation, the journey might seem daunting. However, with the guiding light of Isis, even the most turbulent minds can find solace and clarity.

Isis, the revered goddess of magic and healing, embodies the maternal, nurturing energy that permeates the universe. By invoking her during meditation, we align ourselves with her healing energies, allowing her to guide our inner explorations.

Here's a simple meditation practice to begin your journey:

Setting the Space: Choose a quiet spot, free from distractions. You might light a candle or incense to symbolize Isis's guiding light. Sit comfortably, either on the floor or in a chair, ensuring your spine is straight.

Invoking Isis: Close your eyes and take a deep breath. As you exhale, visualize the radiant energy of Isis enveloping you. Feel her nurturing, protective presence surrounding you. You might silently chant, "Isis, guide me into my inner sanctuary."

Deepening the Meditation: With every inhalation, imagine the golden light of Isis filling you, and with every exhalation, let go of worries and thoughts. Dive deeper into the silence, allowing the goddess's energy to guide you.

Communing in the Sanctuary: As your mind settles, perceive your inner temple's entrance. It might appear as a grand Egyptian temple, a simple room, or even a serene garden. Trust your intuition. Enter this sacred space and feel its tranquility. Here, in the presence of Isis, seek guidance, healing, or simply bask in the silence.

Returning to the Physical Realm: After spending a few minutes (or longer) in your inner sanctuary, gently guide your awareness back to your physical surroundings. Thank Isis for her guidance, slowly open your eyes, and reacquaint yourself with the present moment.

As you practice this meditation regularly, your connection with Isis and your inner temple will strengthen. The once elusive sanctuary of silence will be more accessible, and its wisdom more palpable.

The ancient Egyptians, with their profound wisdom, recognized the sanctity of inner silence and the revelations it could bring. Their practices, though enigmatic, offer us a window into a world where the divine and the mortal intertwined seamlessly. By seeking our inner temple and invoking the nurturing energy of Isis, we too can embark on a transformative journey, tapping into the ancient wellspring of wisdom, healing, and magic.

Chapter 8: Healing Meditation with Isis

The moonlit Nile, a soft silvery glow highlighting its winding path, is more than just a lifeline for Egypt. It is also the spiritual conduit through which the goddess Isis extends her healing embrace. Embarking on a meditation journey with the radiant energy of Isis is like submerging oneself in the waters of this legendary river, feeling its gentle currents washing away our pains and rejuvenating our spirit.

Visualization Techniques

The key to channeling the energy of Isis is through the art of visualization. By painting a mental image that resonates with the essence of the goddess, we can bridge the gap between the physical and spiritual realms.

The Sacred Temple: Begin by finding a quiet space where you won't be disturbed. Sit or lie down comfortably, ensuring your spine is straight and your body relaxed. Close your eyes and take a few deep breaths, grounding yourself in the present moment. Imagine a vast desert landscape stretched out before you. In the distance, you spot a magnificent temple made of gold and adorned with precious gems. As you approach the temple, you realize it's dedicated to Isis, symbolizing your own heart and soul. The temple is your sacred space, a haven where you can connect with the goddess.

River of Light: Within the temple, visualize a stream of pure, white light flowing like the Nile. This river of light represents the love and healing energy of Isis. Dive into the waters and let them cleanse every part of your being. Feel the light entering and healing all wounds, filling you with a warm, radiant glow.

Invoking the Goddess for Healing Energy

Invoking the divine presence of Isis requires a heart full of reverence and a spirit brimming with trust.

The Call: While still immersed in your visualized sanctuary, mentally or audibly chant, "Isis, Great Mother, Healer of All, I invoke your divine presence." Feel her energy enveloping you, as if a gentle, comforting cloak has been draped around your shoulders.

Absorbing Her Essence: As you sense her presence, imagine the goddess standing before you, holding an ankh (the Egyptian key of life). She reaches out and touches your heart center with the ankh. You feel an instant connection, a rush of healing energy coursing through your body. Allow this energy to flow, imagining it targeting areas of pain, distress, or illness, and turning them into light.

Gratitude: After you feel completely rejuvenated, express your gratitude to Isis. It can be a simple "Thank you" or a more elaborate prayer of appreciation. Remember, the bond with the goddess is nurtured through acknowledgment and thanksgiving.

Daily Practices for Continuous Rejuvenation

Integrating the energy of Isis into your daily life can transform mundane routines into rituals of healing and rejuvenation.

Morning Affirmations: Start your day by aligning with the healing energy of Isis. Upon waking, take a deep breath and declare, "Today, I move under the protection and guidance of Isis. Her healing energy surrounds me, filling me with vitality and peace."

Isis Meditation Moments: Dedicate a few minutes every day, preferably during sunrise or sunset, to reconnect with the goddess. This doesn't need to be as elaborate as the full visualization but can be a simple moment of closing your eyes, visualizing the goddess's radiant face, and feeling her energy envelop you.

Sacred Symbols: Surround yourself with symbols associated with Isis. It can be jewelry fashioned in the form of an ankh or winged Isis, or even artwork depicting the goddess. Every time you lay eyes on these symbols, let them be a gentle reminder of the goddess's ever-present healing energy.

Nightly Energy Cleanse: Before drifting into sleep, imagine the River of Light flowing through you, washing away the day's stress and fatigue. Envision the protective wings of Isis wrapped around you, ensuring a night of peaceful, rejuvenating rest.

Incorporating these practices into your life helps you form a deep, unwavering bond with Isis. With time and dedication, the line between the meditator and the goddess begins to blur, leading to a realization that the healing energy of Isis is not external but a profound part of our own being.

In essence, healing meditation with Isis is a transformative journey of self-discovery and rejuvenation. By tapping into the goddess's ancient wisdom and energy, we not only find solace from our afflictions but also uncover an inexhaustible reservoir of strength and vitality within us. Through visualization, invocation, and daily integration, we align ourselves with the benevolent force of Isis, ensuring a life imbued with healing, hope, and harmony.

Chapter 9: The Power of Sacred Rituals

In the heart of ancient Egyptian civilization, rituals served as the cornerstone of daily life, and the mighty Isis stood at the epicenter of these sacred practices. The rituals, from simple daily routines to grand ceremonies, were powerful tools that not only honored the deities but also provided tangible benefits to those who performed them. To truly embrace the teachings of Isis, one must first understand the significance of these rituals and learn to incorporate them into modern life.

Daily routines that honor Isis

The Egyptians didn't perceive a separation between their daily life and the divine. Their mundane routines were seamlessly intertwined with their spiritual practices. By incorporating worship and honor of Isis into daily tasks, they ensured that her energy and guidance remained a continuous force in their lives.

Morning Reverence

In the soft light of dawn, priests and devotees alike would face the east, where the sun began its journey. They would recite hymns that celebrated Isis as the mother, the healer, and the protector. Simple gestures, such as offering a bowl of fresh water or lighting a fragrant incense stick, could serve as an act of devotion. Such rituals were not only acts of worship but were also grounding practices that centered individuals for the day ahead.

Modern practitioners can replicate this by setting aside a few moments every morning to offer gratitude and seek guidance from Isis. Even if it's just a silent acknowledgment while watching the sunrise, these moments can create a deep connection to the deity.

Evening Recollections

As day transitioned into night, individuals would once again turn their attention to the divine. Before bedtime, they would recount their day's events, silently or aloud, offering thanks for the blessings received and seeking solace for any challenges faced.

For contemporary followers, ending the day with a journal entry or a quiet meditation, focusing on Isis's guiding and protective energy, can provide comfort and clarity.

Embracing ceremonies for healing and empowerment

While daily practices brought consistent spiritual connection, there were grand ceremonies dedicated to Isis that dove deep into healing and empowerment. These ceremonies often coincided with lunar cycles, equinoxes, and other astronomical events, maximizing the power of nature and divinity.

One of the most renowned ceremonies was the Feast of Isis, a festival celebrating her as the mother and the creator. Participants would gather by the Nile, where they would embark on a symbolic journey, traveling in boats adorned with lotus flowers. Songs and dances filled the air as the community celebrated the goddess's benevolence.

To replicate such profound ceremonies, one doesn't need to organize grand feasts or river journeys. Organizing a gathering during a significant lunar phase, such as the full moon or new moon, can suffice. A simple circle of trusted individuals, sharing stories, singing hymns dedicated to Isis, and perhaps performing a symbolic gesture like lighting a communal candle, can invoke her power.

Crafting your own healing rituals

The beauty of rituals lies in their adaptability. While traditional practices provide a strong foundation, the real power emerges when individuals craft rituals that resonate with their unique life experiences and needs.

Identifying the Purpose

Every ritual should have a clear purpose. Whether it's seeking guidance, expressing gratitude, invoking protection, or attaining healing, understanding the intent ensures the energy is directed appropriately.

Creating a Sacred Space

The surroundings play a significant role in amplifying the ritual's energy. This doesn't necessarily mean building grand altars; even a small corner of a room, adorned with symbols and artifacts that resonate with the practitioner's relationship with Isis, can serve as a potent space.

Selecting Symbols and Offerings

Symbols like the ankh, the winged disc, and the lotus flower are closely associated with Isis. Incorporating these into rituals can invoke her essence. Offerings such as fresh flowers, pure water, or even written notes of gratitude can form an integral part of the ritual.

Crafting the Ritual

With all elements in place, the next step is to design the ritual. It can be as simple as lighting a candle while reciting a hymn, or as elaborate as an hour-long meditation session where one visualizes journeying through ancient Egyptian landscapes, seeking Isis's guidance.

Closing rituals with a word or gesture of gratitude not only completes the cycle but also anchors the benefits received.

Rituals, both daily and ceremonial, serve as bridges between the mortal realm and the divine. By embracing these sacred practices, one doesn't just honor Isis but also taps into an ancient source of healing, empowerment, and wisdom. It's a journey of deepening one's connection to the cosmos, guided by the loving and protective embrace of Isis.

Chapter 10: Embracing Nature's Cycles

The passage of time, with its ever-changing seasons, tides, and lunar phases, stands as a profound testament to the cyclical nature of life. Just as nature experiences regeneration, death, rebirth, and growth, so do we. Embracing these natural cycles allows us to understand the ebbs and flows of our own lives, leading us towards holistic healing and alignment with our true selves.

The understanding of these cycles is not a new phenomenon. Ancient civilizations, including the

Egyptians, based their lives around them, marking time with the seasons, moon phases, and the great Nile's inundation. Among these, the deity Isis stood out, a maternal goddess symbolizing rebirth and regeneration, closely associated with the moon and tides. Her tales and teachings offer timeless wisdom on aligning with these cycles for a deeper, more profound healing experience.

Understanding the Cyclical Nature of Life and Healing

Cycles surround us. They are in the day turning to night, the budding of flowers come spring, and the shedding of leaves in autumn. They are in our own lives too: childhood, adolescence, adulthood, and old age. Our bodies, too, have their own rhythms — from the cellular level, where cells regenerate, to the more evident cycles of sleep, hunger, and even emotional highs and lows.

This cyclical nature is a reminder that nothing is permanent. Pain and suffering are transient, as are joy and happiness. The acceptance of this can bring a unique kind of peace. When we understand that moments of despair will pass, we can endure with greater resilience. And when we realize moments of joy are fleeting, we learn to cherish them more.

But there's another layer to this cyclical understanding. By aligning with these cycles, we can harness their energies for our healing. When we act in tandem with nature, we reduce resistance and enhance our ability to heal, grow, and transform.

Isis' Association with the Moon and Tides

The luminous moon, with its waxing and waning, was a significant symbol in ancient Egyptian cosmology. It represented rebirth and regeneration, a dance of growing and receding energies, perfectly mirroring life on earth. Isis, with her tales of death and resurrection, particularly in the story of Osiris, is deeply intertwined with the moon's symbolism.

Isis was often depicted with the horns of a cow cradling a moon disk, symbolizing her connection with the moon's nurturing and cyclical aspects. Her association was not just symbolic. It was believed that Isis, with her magical powers, could even regulate the moon's course, control the tides, and ensure the Nile's annual flooding, which was essential for Egypt's fertility.

The tides, guided by the moon's pull, also hold a deeper meaning. Just as the tides ebb and flow, so do the circumstances of our lives. There are moments of high energy, symbolized by the high tide, and moments of retreat and introspection, symbolized by the low tide. Isis, with her moon associations, becomes the guiding force, teaching us to harness these natural rhythms for our own growth and healing.

Aligning with Nature for Deeper Healing

Embracing the cycles of nature isn't merely an act of observation; it's an active alignment. Here's how one can synchronize with these natural rhythms for deeper healing:

Tune Into Lunar Cycles: Just as the ancient Egyptians did, observe the phases of the moon. New moons are a time for introspection and setting intentions. Full moons, with their illuminating energy, are ideal for manifestation and bringing projects to fruition. By aligning our actions with these phases, we tap into a reservoir of natural energy.

Seasonal Alignment: Each season brings its own energy. Spring is a time for new beginnings, while winter is a period of retreat and reflection. By adjusting our activities, diet, and even our healing practices with the seasons, we flow with nature, not against it.

Acknowledge Personal Cycles: Every individual has their rhythms. By understanding and respecting our personal cycles of energy, emotion, and even health, we can provide ourselves with what we need when we need it, facilitating better healing and growth.

Meditate with Nature: Incorporating elements of nature into meditation, be it the sound of waves, the rustling of leaves, or simply meditating under the moonlight, can intensify the healing experience. This practice not only grounds us but also enhances our connection to the greater cosmos.

Seek Lessons from Isis: Dive deep into the myths and teachings of Isis. Through her stories, one can gather timeless wisdom on resilience, rebirth, and the importance of aligning with natural cycles.

Nature, with its cyclical rhythms, offers a mirror to our own lives, reminding us of the impermanence of all things and the potential for rebirth and regeneration. Isis, as a beacon of these natural cycles, teaches us to navigate the rhythms of life with grace, resilience, and an understanding that healing, like nature, is a continuous journey. By aligning ourselves with these cycles, we not only enhance our healing processes but also cultivate a deeper connection with the world around us and the cosmos at large.

Chapter 11: The Alchemy of Emotions

The shifting sands of Egypt mirror the ever-evolving landscape of human emotions. Just as the deserts have their storms and the Nile has its ebbs and flows, so do our feelings. The ancient Egyptians, with their profound understanding of the universe's rhythms, recognized the transformative potential of emotions. At the heart of these teachings stood the goddess Isis, a beacon of strength and resilience.

Transforming Pain into Power

Pain, often viewed as an unwanted companion, has been an intrinsic part of the human experience. While it's natural to shun pain or suppress it, doing so merely pushes it into the shadows, from where it can exert unseen influence over our lives. The teachings of Isis show us another way: to confront our pain and transform it into a source of strength.

In the myths of Isis, her pain was palpable. She experienced the loss of her husband Osiris, was forced into hiding to protect her son, and had to piece together her shattered life. Yet, she never faltered. Instead, she used her pain as a fuel, a motivating force that powered her magic and determination. Her story illustrates that pain, when embraced, can be alchemized into power.

The initial step in this transformation is acknowledgment. Recognize the pain, give it a voice, and allow it its space. Much like a wound exposed to air begins to heal, emotions, when recognized, start their journey from raw pain to healing power. It's essential not to rush this process; the transformation happens in its own time.

Using Emotions as Catalysts for Change and Healing

Every emotion we experience, whether positive or negative, holds a lesson. Happiness teaches us about the things that resonate with our soul, while sadness sheds light on areas of our life that need change. Anger can spotlight injustice, while love can show us the beauty in connection.

To see emotions as catalysts, we must first stop judging them. Society often categorizes feelings into 'good' or 'bad', but in the eyes of the ancients, and certainly for Isis, every emotion was valid. They were all part of the rich tapestry of the human experience.

Once we see our emotions without judgment, we can begin to ask what they're trying to tell us. For instance, prolonged feelings of discontent might signal the need for change in certain areas of our lives. Instead of suppressing this discontent, we can harness it, allowing it to propel us forward towards positive change.

Furthermore, emotions can be powerful tools for healing. Grief, for instance, when processed, can lead to profound personal growth. It can deepen our empathy, enriching our connections with others. Fear, when confronted, can become a stepping stone to courage.

The Emotional Teachings of Isis

Isis, in her wisdom, offers profound teachings on emotions. Firstly, she exemplifies the power of vulnerability. In her quest to find the scattered pieces of Osiris, she showed raw emotion, weeping and lamenting. Yet, her vulnerability was not a sign of weakness; it was a testament to her strength. Through her, we learn that embracing our emotions, in all their raw intensity, is an act of courage.

Isis also teaches us about the importance of patience in the emotional realm. In her stories, she often had to wait, whether it was for the right moment to act or for her magic to take effect. Similarly, our emotions often require patience. Healing doesn't happen overnight, and sometimes, our feelings need time to evolve and shift.

Lastly, the goddess emphasizes the importance of support. Throughout her trials, Isis sought the help of other deities and beings. This highlights the significance of seeking support during emotionally challenging times, be it from friends, family, or professionals.

Emotions, in all their complexity, are neither our enemies nor obstacles. They are, in fact, guideposts, signaling the path we should take or changes we need to make. The stories and teachings of Isis illuminate the ways in which we can harness our feelings, transforming them from sources of pain to reservoirs of strength.

The alchemy of emotions isn't about turning negative feelings into positive ones. It's about understanding the inherent value in every emotion, seeing each one as a teacher and guide. As we journey through life, with Isis as our guiding star, we can begin to embrace the full spectrum of our emotional experience, finding healing, strength, and wisdom along the way.

Chapter 12: Cultivating Resilience through Community

The story of human resilience often starts and ends with community. From the deep-seated tribal networks of our ancestors to the interconnected digital communities of today, we've always looked to one another for strength, solace, and shared understanding. In the world of ancient Egypt, this communal bond was epitomized in the gatherings held in honor of the goddess Isis.

Ancient Gatherings in Honor of Isis

Isis, known as the goddess of healing, magic, and protection, was revered not just for her divine prowess but also for the communal spirit she embodied. As the stories go, she wandered the earth in search of her husband Osiris's body parts, showcasing an incredible resilience and determination. Her journey was not solitary; wherever she went, she forged connections, imparting wisdom and teaching the secrets of healing.

To honor this revered deity, ancient Egyptians organized grand ceremonies and gatherings. These were not just rituals; they were community events, drawing people from various walks of life. They sang hymns in honor of Isis, conducted processions, and shared tales of her feats. Temples dedicated to Isis became hubs of social and spiritual connection. It was common for people to travel long distances, often on foot, just to be a part of these gatherings.

The very act of congregating in her honor was in itself a form of collective healing. People exchanged stories of their own trials and tribulations, drawing parallels with Isis's journey and seeking solace in shared experiences. The idea was simple: If Isis, despite her divine stature, faced adversities and emerged stronger, so could they. And together, as a community, they could amplify this strength manifold.

Building a Community of Healers in Modern Times

The modern world, with its skyscrapers, technology, and digital realms, might seem far removed from the deserts of ancient Egypt. Yet, the essence of community remains unchanged. Today, more than ever, we realize the importance of connection, of shared stories, and the power of collective resilience.

In this age of information, communities are no longer restricted by geography. Digital platforms have given rise to global communities where individuals, irrespective of their location, come together driven by a shared purpose or interest. In the realm of healing, such digital communities have taken on a role akin to the ancient gatherings in honor of Isis.

Imagine online forums, dedicated groups, and virtual sessions where individuals from around the world share their journeys of healing and transformation. These are our modern temples, dedicated to resilience, hope, and shared growth.

Just as in ancient times, stories are exchanged, experiences are shared, and wisdom is imparted.

Building a community of healers in today's era begins with recognizing the shared human experience. It's about creating spaces - digital or physical - where stories of healing, transformation, and resilience can be shared without judgment. Such communities become sanctuaries of hope, guiding individuals through their darkest hours, much like the guiding light of Isis for the ancient Egyptians.

The Strength of Collective Healing

There's a profound power in shared experiences. It's one thing to journey through adversity alone, but to know that there are others who have faced similar challenges and emerged stronger provides an unparalleled strength.

Collective healing is built on this foundation of shared stories and experiences. It's a synergy of individual resilience. When a community comes together, be it in the shadow of a temple dedicated to Isis or in a modern-day healing forum, the combined energies foster an environment conducive to healing and growth.

There's also an element of collective wisdom. Every individual, through their journey, acquires unique insights, strategies, and coping mechanisms. When such knowledge is pooled together, it becomes a reservoir of wisdom, accessible to anyone in need. This was evident in the ancient gatherings where tales of Isis's wisdom were shared, and it's evident today in communities where personal stories of triumph over adversity inspire countless others. The strength of collective healing lies in the community's ability to amplify individual resilience. It's a reflection of the timeless adage — together we stand strong. And in this collective strength, we find echoes of the ancient world, of gatherings in honor of Isis, and a testament to the enduring power of human connection. Whether in the ancient sands of Egypt or the digital landscapes of today, the concept of community remains a beacon of hope and resilience. It's a reminder that we are not alone in our journey, and together, as a collective, we have the power to heal, grow, and transform. As we move forward, let us remember the lessons from the past and harness the power of community, cultivating resilience and ensuring that the spirit of collective healing, epitomized by Isis, lives on.

Chapter 13: Healing through Sacred Music and Dance

Throughout the annals of time, human civilizations have resorted to music and dance as channels of expression, celebration, mourning, and healing. The Ancient Egyptians, with their advanced understanding of aesthetics and spirituality, were no different. Central to their musical reverence was the goddess Isis, the embodiment of healing and magic.

Ancient Egyptian Music: An Ode to Isis

The music of ancient Egypt was a harmonious blend of rhythm, melody, and purpose. Instruments like the sistrum (a type of rattle), lyres, harps, and flutes dominated the musical soundscape. Among these, the sistrum held particular significance in the worship of Isis. Not just an instrument, it was considered sacred to her, symbolizing her capacity to drive away evil spirits and bring forth prosperity and health.

In the grand temples dedicated to Isis, the gentle hum of hymns in her honor often filled the air. These hymns, rich with emotion, spoke of her exploits, her kindness, and her healing prowess. They were more than mere songs; they were prayers, invocations, and spells aimed at drawing her attention and favor.

Dancers, usually priestesses of the temple, swayed to these hymns. Their movements were fluid, echoing the flow of the Nile, symbolizing both life's transient nature and the timeless power of Isis. Their dance was an offering, a manifestation of gratitude, and a plea for her blessings.

Rhythm and Motion: Tools of Catharsis

The rhythmic patterns of Egyptian music, combined with the hypnotic swirls and twirls of the dancers, had a profound effect on the psyche. It was as if the beats resonated with the heart's own rhythms, while the dance mirrored the soul's deepest desires and fears.

For an observer or participant, this experience was incredibly cathartic. Through the music and dance, emotions locked deep within were set free, allowed to surface, be acknowledged, and then released. Anguish transformed into tears, joy into laughter, and fear into a rush of adrenaline. This emotional release, achieved through the synergy of rhythm and motion, was a therapeutic process.

The dances were often communal, blurring the lines between the dancers and the observers. Everyone present became part of the ritual. This collective energy magnified the emotional release, turning individual catharsis into a shared experience of healing and rejuvenation.

Healing through Resonance

Music and dance have an innate ability to resonate with our internal frequencies. Ancient Egyptians, with their keen sense of spirituality, realized that every emotion, every thought, and every ailment had its own vibration. By introducing an external frequency through music, especially one that was in harmony with the goddess of healing, they believed they could alter the internal frequencies, pushing the negative out and allowing the positive to take precedence.

It's a principle that's not too far removed from today's sound therapy or rhythmic breathing practices. The core idea remains: by aligning our internal rhythms with external healing frequencies, we achieve balance and health.

Integrating Sacred Music and Dance into Modern Life

While we live in a world vastly different from ancient Egypt, the fundamental human emotions remain unchanged. The need for expression, connection, and healing is as relevant today as it was millennia ago.

To integrate these age-old practices into our daily life, we need not build temples or compose hymns. Here's how we can begin:

Creating a Sacred Space: Dedicate a quiet corner of your home for music and movement. Fill it with elements that resonate with you - perhaps a simple rug, candles, or even a picture of Isis.

Curated Music: The internet is a treasure trove of ancient Egyptian-inspired music. While the original hymns might be lost to time, many artists have recreated what they believe the music might have sounded like. Play this in your sacred space.

Move Freely: You don't need to know the exact dance steps from the era. The objective is emotional release. Close your eyes and move as the music guides you. Feel the beats, let them guide your heart, and allow your body to express what words cannot.

Group Sessions: Just as the ancient Egyptians practiced communal healing, invite friends or join groups that focus on dance as therapy. There's a unique power in collective healing.

Regular Practice: Healing is not a one-time activity. Just as our ancestors integrated music and dance into their daily worship and life, we must make it a part of our routine. Even a few minutes a day can make a significant difference.

While we might be separated by time and culture from the ancient Egyptians, the wisdom of their practices remains available to us. By embracing the healing power of music and dance, and by recognizing the divine resonance it shares with our very souls, we can walk a path of emotional freedom, wellness, and profound connection with the energies that surround us. The rhythms of the past, infused with the spirit of Isis, can guide our hearts today.

Chapter 14: The Power of Symbols and Amulets

The sands of ancient Egypt whisper tales of powerful pharaohs, massive pyramids, and the Nile's life-giving waters. But more subtly, they speak of secrets carried by symbols and amulets that held a spiritual and protective significance that transcends time. These were not mere ornamental pieces, but vessels of potent energies and intentions, designed to safeguard, heal, and empower. The ancient Egyptians were profound believers in the power of symbols and the efficacy of amulets. For them, the boundary between the physical and metaphysical worlds was thin, and it was through symbols and talismans that they bridged the gap.

Egyptian Talismans and Their Meanings

At the core of Egyptian cosmology were symbols that represented fundamental truths about the universe. These symbols could be seen etched on temple walls, carved into statues, and worn as amulets around the necks of both the elite and the commoners.

The Ankh, often referred to as the "key of life", is one of the most recognizable Egyptian symbols. It symbolizes life itself and the essence of mortality intertwined with divinity. Pharaohs are often depicted holding the Ankh, drawing a direct connection between their earthly rule and divine favor.

The Eye of Horus, or the Wadjet, is a symbol of protection, health, and restoration. Derived from the story where Horus lost his eye in a battle with Set, only to have it restored, it reminds us of the resilience of the human spirit and the potential for recovery and healing.

The Scarab beetle represented transformation and regeneration. Ancient Egyptians believed that the scarab renewed the sun every day before rolling it above the horizon, then carrying it through the other world after sunset, only to renew it, again, the next day.

And then there was the Djed column, symbolizing stability, strength, and the god Osiris. It is believed to represent Osiris's spine, around which his body was wrapped and then resurrected.

Each of these symbols wasn't merely a representation; it was a conduit of the energy it signified. When crafted into amulets and worn, they channeled the energies they epitomized, offering protection, power, or favor to their bearer.

Creating Your Own Protective and Healing Amulets

While the power of ancient amulets is undeniable, there's a unique strength in crafting your own talisman, infusing it with your intent, energy, and purpose. When making your own amulet, it's essential to keep in mind the symbolic significance, the materials used, and the intentions you pour into it.

Begin by selecting the right material. Ancient Egyptians often used stones, metals, clay, or faience (a ceramic material) for their amulets. Each material resonated with a specific vibration. For instance, lapis lazuli was prized for its heavenly connection, while carnelian was seen as a source of vitality and strength.

Carve or mold your chosen symbol into your chosen material. As you do this, be in a meditative state, channeling your purpose and intent into your creation.

Once your amulet is shaped, cleanse it. This could be done using sacred smoke from sage, immersing it in the light of the moon, or using the vibrations of sound from bells or chimes. This step is to ensure that any extraneous energies are purged.

Finally, consecrate your amulet. Hold it close to your heart, close your eyes, and envision the energy of Isis, radiant and resplendent, flowing into the amulet. Feel her protection, her strength, her wisdom enveloping it. Seal this process with a prayer or affirmation that encapsulates your intention.

Channeling the Energy of Isis through Sacred Objects

Channeling the energy of Isis isn't limited to merely wearing an amulet. Sacred objects like statues, sacred jewelry, or even inscribed scrolls can become conduits of her divine energy.

To draw upon Isis' energy through a sacred object, it needs to be consecrated in her name. Place the object on an altar dedicated to her, adorned with white and gold fabrics, and surrounded by candles and offerings. Offerings could be fresh flowers, incense, or even a bowl of water representing the Nile.

Invoke Isis through a chant or prayer, asking her to bless the object and infuse it with her essence. As you do this, imagine a cascade of brilliant white light, tinged with gold, descending upon the object, making it radiant and alive with her energy.

Keep this object in a sacred space, and whenever you need the guidance, strength, or protection of Isis, hold it close, feel its energy, and let her wisdom guide you.

Symbols and amulets serve as physical reminders of the spiritual truths and energies that permeate our universe.

By understanding their significance, crafting them with intent, and consecrating them with divine energy, we can harness their profound power to heal, protect, and guide us in our journey.

Whether ancient or modern, these talismans continue to bridge the gap between the seen and the unseen, anchoring us to the vast cosmos and its myriad mysteries.

Chapter 15: Nurturing the Soul: Diet and Well-being

Ancient Egyptian Dietary Practices

The Nile, that majestic river which graces the heart of Egypt, has been the lifeblood of its civilization for millennia. It isn't just a source of water, but also the cornerstone upon which ancient Egyptian dietary practices were built. Agriculture thrived on the fertile banks of the Nile, and the river itself teemed with fish, providing sustenance to the populace.

Cereals, primarily emmer wheat and barley, formed the foundation of the ancient Egyptian diet. These grains were used to make bread and beer, staples in almost every household regardless of social status. The bread was usually round and flat, sometimes flavored with ingredients like dates or herbs.

Vegetables were abundant, especially onions, garlic, leeks, lentils, and chickpeas. They believed garlic and onions possessed health-giving properties, possibly because of their effectiveness in warding off various infections, a fact acknowledged by modern science today.

While vegetables and cereals were dietary mainstays, fruits like dates, figs, and pomegranates were highly treasured, not just for their sweetness but also for their symbolic associations with fertility and rebirth.

The Nile yielded a variety of fish, making it a significant source of protein. However, while fish was widely consumed, especially in the settlements closer to the river, the consumption of meat was more selective. Poultry like ducks and geese were relatively common, but red meat, primarily from cattle, goats, and sheep, was considered a luxury, more commonly found in the diets of the elite or during special occasions.

Foods Sacred to Isis

As the goddess of motherhood, magic, and fertility, Isis had a special connection to certain foods that symbolized life, rejuvenation, and health.

The date palm, for instance, was seen as the tree of life in ancient Egyptian mythology. Its fruit, the date, was linked with Isis due to its sweet, life-giving properties. Consumed fresh or dried, dates were considered a source of energy and vitality.

Another food sacred to Isis was the pomegranate. With its numerous seeds and rich, blood-red color, it became a symbol of fertility and abundance. Its associations with rebirth and the cycles of life made it particularly apt for Isis, who was revered for bringing her husband Osiris back from the dead.

Emmer wheat, too, had its ties to the goddess. This grain, vital for bread-making, was seen as a gift from Isis, nourishing the Egyptian people both physically and spiritually. During certain rituals and festivals dedicated to Isis, bread made from emmer wheat would be ceremoniously offered to her, a token of gratitude for the sustenance she provided.

Milk and dairy products, reminiscent of maternal nourishment, were also connected with Isis. Fresh milk, cheese, and butter were considered blessings from the goddess, symbolizing nurturing, growth, and abundance.

Crafting a Diet That Nourishes Both Body and Soul

While the ancient Egyptians didn't have the scientific knowledge we possess today about nutrition, they intuitively understood the connection between food, well-being, and spiritual health. To craft a diet that nourishes both body and soul, we can draw inspiration from their practices and the foods they held sacred.

Whole Grains: Just as emmer wheat and barley were staples in ancient Egypt, incorporate whole grains like quinoa, millet, and oats into your diet. They are not only nutritionally rich but also provide sustained energy.

Fresh Produce: Embrace a variety of vegetables and fruits, especially those with deep colors like the pomegranate. These foods are rich in antioxidants, which combat cellular damage.

Fish and Lean Proteins: Drawing from the Nile's bounty, include fish, especially those rich in omega-3 fatty acids like salmon and mackerel, in your diet. Complement this with other lean proteins like poultry.

Limit Red Meat: While red meat was a luxury in ancient Egypt, modern studies suggest excessive consumption can be detrimental to health. Instead, view it as they did: a treat to be enjoyed occasionally.

Natural Sweeteners: Instead of processed sugars, turn to natural sweeteners like dates or honey. They not only provide a touch of sweetness but also contain essential minerals and nutrients.

Stay Hydrated: The Nile was the heart of Egyptian civilization, underscoring the importance of water. Drink plenty of water, and if you wish, occasionally flavor it with fresh herbs or fruits for added benefits.

Mindful Eating: Beyond the physical aspects of food, nourishing the soul is about intention and mindfulness. Take the time to savor each bite, express gratitude for your meal, and recognize the energy it imparts.

As we draw inspiration from Isis and the dietary practices of ancient Egypt, we're reminded that food is more than just sustenance. It's a bridge between the physical and spiritual, a means to connect with the divine and the cycles of nature. By honoring these principles and the sacred foods associated with the goddess, we craft a diet that truly nurtures both body and soul.

Chapter 16: Merging with the Cosmos: The Stellar Aspect of Isis

In the annals of ancient Egyptian mythology, where gods and goddesses adorned the stories as archetypes of nature's forces and moral compasses, the story of Isis stands out. Not just as a tale of power and magic, but as a cosmic narrative deeply interwoven with the universe. Her association with the stars, particularly the constellation of Sirius, is both poetic and profound, symbolizing her omnipresence and undying influence on the Egyptian psyche and their worldview.

Isis and her Association with the Stars

The ancients viewed the night sky not just as a mesmerizing tapestry of twinkling lights, but as a map, a canvas upon which tales of gods and men were painted. For the Egyptians, the brightest star in the sky, Sirius, also known as the Dog Star, held particular significance. This star was, in many stories and rituals, closely linked to Isis.

Sirius, known to Egyptians as 'Sopdet,' makes its first appearance in the eastern sky just before the dawn, heralding the coming inundation of the Nile. This annual event was of immeasurable importance, signifying both renewal and the divine connection of the heavens with the Earth. Isis, in her vast roles, was the goddess of fertility and rebirth, and the rising of Sirius, signaling the Nile's flood, was intertwined with her mythos.

In essence, the star became a celestial symbol of Isis herself. Just as the Nile would bring fertility and sustenance to the land, Isis, associated with Sirius, brought life, hope, and renewal to the cosmos and her followers.

Aligning with Cosmic Energies for Healing

Beyond mere tales and mythologies, the association of Isis with Sirius carried deeper spiritual implications. For Egyptians, this alignment between a deity and a celestial body was a clear testament to the belief that the cosmos directly influenced life on Earth. It meant that by tuning into these cosmic energies, especially those associated with Isis, one could attain healing, guidance, and a deeper understanding of one's place in the universe.

Healing, in the traditional Egyptian context, was not merely a physical act. It was an alignment of the body, mind, and soul. The energies of the cosmos, as brought forth by stars and particularly by Sirius, were believed to be channels of potent spiritual power. The followers of Isis would often engage in nighttime rituals, seeking her blessings and guidance, with Sirius shining brightly above. They believed that under its luminescent gaze, the veil between the divine and mortal realms thinned, allowing for a free flow of cosmic energies.

These energies, when harnessed correctly, could rejuvenate the spirit, cleanse past traumas, and provide clarity in thought and purpose. The star's annual appearance, especially, was a time of heightened spiritual activity, with many seeking the curative and protective embrace of Isis.

Meditative Practices to Connect with the Celestial

Meditation, while universally recognized, held a special place in the practices of ancient Egyptians, especially those devoted to Isis. For them, it was more than just a means to calm the mind; it was a bridge to the cosmos.

A common practice was the 'Stellar Meditation,' wherein the practitioner would focus intently on Sirius, imagining its light descending and enveloping them. This light, imbued with the essence of Isis, would be visualized as a cocoon, healing wounds, and reinvigorating the spirit.

Here's a step-by-step guide to this ancient practice:

Preparation: Choose a quiet place under the open sky, preferably where Sirius is clearly visible.

Grounding: Sit comfortably, either on the ground or on a cushion, maintaining a straight posture. Begin by taking deep, rhythmic breaths, feeling every inhalation and exhalation, grounding yourself in the present moment.

Focus on Sirius: Gently shift your gaze to Sirius, observing its bright luminescence without straining your eyes. Recognize it as the embodiment of Isis in the vast cosmos.

Visualization: Close your eyes and visualize the light from Sirius descending towards you, a radiant beam connecting the star to your heart center. Imagine this light, filled with the nurturing energy of Isis, enveloping your entire being.

Absorption: Feel the light seep into you, healing physical pains, alleviating emotional burdens, and illuminating the mind. Embrace the cosmic connection, the merging of your spirit with the celestial.

Gratitude: As you feel a sense of completeness, take a few moments to express silent gratitude to Isis and the cosmos for this union.

Return: Gently bring your awareness back to your surroundings, taking deep breaths. When ready, open your eyes.

This meditative practice, deeply rooted in the worship and teachings associated with Isis, was believed to forge a bond between the practitioner and the vast universe. It emphasized the belief that every individual, much like the stars, radiates their unique light.

The stellar aspect of Isis offers not just an understanding of ancient Egyptian cosmology but provides pathways for personal healing and growth. By recognizing the interplay between the divine, the cosmos, and oneself, it becomes evident that healing is not just an inward journey but an expansive voyage into the universe's very heart, guided by the luminous energy of Isis.

Chapter 17: The Role of Sacred Waters

The story of water, particularly of the Nile, is deeply intertwined with the narrative of the Egyptian goddess Isis. This life-giving river, which ebbs and flows through the heart of Egypt, is more than just a waterway. For the ancients, it was the very lifeblood of their civilization and held a divine connection with Isis herself. In this chapter, we shall dive deep into the significance of the Nile in Isis' tales, explore the use of water in healing rituals and practices, and discover the transformative power of sacred waters.

The Nile: A River of Life and Legends

The Nile has always been a central figure in Egyptian life. Its annual inundation brought not just water but life, ensuring fertile lands and a prosperous civilization. However, beyond its material benefits, the Nile held profound spiritual significance, often being linked with Isis, one of Egypt's most venerated deities.

One of the most poignant tales involving Isis and the Nile is her relentless search for her husband Osiris' body parts, scattered by his jealous brother Seth. The legend narrates how Seth, envious of Osiris' prosperity and rule, plotted to kill him. After succeeding in his nefarious plot, Seth dismembered Osiris's body and scattered it across Egypt. Devastated by her loss, Isis roamed the lands, searching every corner, every waterway, and every stretch of the Nile to find her beloved. The Nile, in this tale, serves as both a backdrop and a guide. As Isis journeyed along its banks, the river whispered secrets, offered solace, and even aided her in her quest.

This narrative is not just a story of love and separation but is symbolic of renewal, resurrection, and the eternal cycle of life and death. The Nile's waters, which carried the remnants of Osiris, reflect the ever-continuing cycle of life, transformation, and renewal, themes recurrently associated with Isis.

Water in Healing Rituals and Practices

Water, given its purifying and life-giving qualities, naturally found its place in various healing rituals in ancient Egypt. For the Egyptians, water was not merely H2O; it was a conduit of energy, a medium that could cleanse, renew, and heal.

Temples dedicated to Isis often stood close to the Nile or other water bodies. The sacred pool or the 'Isheru,' usually present in such temples, was not just for decorative purposes. Initiates and seekers would often wade into these waters or be sprinkled with its essence during specific ceremonies, signifying purification and initiation into the mysteries of Isis.

One of the most vital water-related practices was the 'Netjeri,' where sacred water, after being charged with the energies of specific deities, was used for both physical and spiritual cleansing. It was believed that such water had the power to wash away impurities, sickness, and even malevolent energies.

Isis, with her deep association with magic and healing, was often invoked during such rituals. Priests and priestesses would chant her sacred hymns, calling upon her energy to infuse the water, turning it into a potent elixir of health, protection, and rejuvenation.

Embracing the Cleansing Properties of Sacred Waters

Beyond rituals, the concept of water as a cleanser for both body and soul has been prevalent across many cultures. For followers of Isis, the act of connecting with water was a profound spiritual practice.

Simple acts, like washing hands or taking a bath, were not just about physical cleanliness. When done with intention and reverence, these became acts of spiritual cleansing, where one not only washed away the grime of the day but also let go of negative energies, intrusive thoughts, and emotional burdens.

Isis' followers were often encouraged to meditate by the banks of the Nile or any water body. The rhythmic sound of flowing water, they believed, had a calming effect on the mind, helping the seeker attune to deeper spiritual truths.

They were also taught the art of 'water gazing' – a meditative practice where one would gaze deeply into a water body, letting its depths reveal visions, insights, and even prophecies. The reflection of the moon on the Nile's waters during the night was considered especially powerful for this practice.

Water, especially the sacred waters of the Nile, held a place of reverence in the lore and practices associated with Isis. It was seen as a medium of transformation, a conduit of divine energy, and a symbol of the eternal cycles of life, death, and rebirth. As we navigate through our lives, recognizing and honoring the sacredness of water can offer healing, solace, and a deeper connection with the divine, just as it did for the ancients who walked the banks of the Nile, whispering their prayers to Isis.

Chapter 18: Unveiling the Shadows

In the vibrant tapestry of the human soul, there is a delicate interplay between light and darkness. This dichotomy isn't exclusive to the human psyche; it has been recognized and explored in various cultures and spiritual traditions, ancient and modern alike. The ancient Egyptians, with their profound understanding of duality, were no exception. Central to their cosmology was the goddess Isis, whose narratives and teachings offer invaluable insights into unveiling and integrating our shadows.

The term "shadow" in psychological parlance refers to the unconscious part of our personality that contains repressed weaknesses, desires, and instincts. It's our darker self, lurking beneath the surface, manifesting in moments of anger, jealousy, and other emotions we might prefer to deny. But to perceive the shadow merely as a negative force would be an oversimplification. It also contains latent talents and strengths, awaiting recognition.

Exploring the Shadow Side and Its Role in Healing

Diving into the depths of our own psyche might be an intimidating venture, but it is essential for holistic healing. Embracing the shadow side does not mean surrendering to our basest instincts but understanding them. When we confront our shadows, we take a pivotal step towards self-awareness.

The ancient Egyptian tales, rife with tales of battles and reconciliations, are allegorical representations of this internal struggle. Take, for example, the story of Isis and her quest to retrieve and restore the scattered parts of her beloved Osiris. This narrative can be seen as an allegory for piecing together the fragmented parts of ourselves, including those that lurk in the shadows.

In her journey, Isis had to confront Set, the god of chaos, storms, and disorder. Set, in this context, embodies the shadow, the chaotic and unpredictable part of our nature. But Isis's approach was neither of outright confrontation nor total avoidance. She demonstrated a keen understanding of the balance between light and darkness, teaching us that one cannot exist without the other. To heal wholly, as Isis sought to restore Osiris, we must recognize and integrate our shadow.

Lessons from Isis on Balancing Light and Darkness

Isis, with her dual wings of light and shadow, exemplifies balance. Her tales emphasize the importance of harmonizing the contrasting facets of our being. Here are some lessons from her:

Acceptance: Before any form of integration, there must be acceptance. Isis did not deny the existence of Set or the darkness he represented. Likewise, we must accept that our shadow self exists, acknowledging its presence without judgment.

Understanding: Once acknowledged, seek to understand the origins of these shadows. Many of our fears, insecurities, and repressed desires stem from past experiences. By understanding their origins, we can address the root causes, not just the symptoms.

Transformation: The shadow, once illuminated, loses its power over us. Isis teaches us that with patience, love, and magic, chaos can be transformed. In personal terms, this means utilizing self-awareness and understanding to transform our darker instincts into strengths.

Techniques to Integrate and Heal Your Shadow Self

Shadow Journaling: Begin by writing down moments when you felt intense emotions such as anger, jealousy, or shame. Reflect on the triggers and try to understand the deeper reasons behind these feelings. Over time, patterns will emerge, allowing you to identify recurring shadow aspects.

Meditation: A guided visualization where you confront and converse with your shadow can be revealing. Imagine walking in a dimly lit room where your shadow self-resides. Engage with it.

Ask questions. This exercise can offer profound insights into the unconscious mind.

Art Therapy: Expressing your shadow through art can be both cathartic and enlightening. Paint, sketch, or sculpt, allowing your instincts to guide you. The colors and shapes you gravitate towards can shed light on the nature of your shadow.

Dream Analysis: The shadow often communicates through dreams. Maintain a dream journal. Over time, you'll begin to understand the symbols and patterns representing your shadow aspects.

Seek Professional Guidance: A trained therapist or counselor can provide valuable tools and techniques to help you navigate and integrate your shadow.

Unveiling the shadows is a continuous journey of introspection and self-discovery. As we delve deeper, we find that the line between light and shadow is not as distinct as it might seem. The duality exists in harmony, each aspect giving depth and dimension to the other. As the great goddess Isis showcases in her tales and teachings, embracing and balancing both these facets is the true path to holistic healing and self-realization.

Chapter 19: The Continuous Journey of Healing

In the shifting sands of time, the lessons from ancient Egypt still ripple through our modern understanding, reminding us of truths we've known but perhaps forgotten. One such truth, immortalized through the tales and teachings of the great goddess Isis, is the reality of healing as an ongoing journey.

Recognizing Healing as a Never-Ending Journey

Healing, contrary to popular belief, is not a destination. It is a path, winding and varied, with its plateaus, valleys, and peaks. Like a river that constantly flows, carving its way through mountains and plains, healing is perpetual, always moving, always evolving.

In our instant-gratification society, we often search for quick fixes. We desire immediate relief from pain, immediate resolution of issues, and immediate attainment of wellness. However, true healing, the kind that touches the soul and transforms the essence, is a continuous process. It's a series of tiny steps and adjustments, of understanding and realizations, of letting go and embracing.

Each moment presents us with opportunities to heal — from past traumas, from present challenges, and from the fears of an uncertain future. The realization that healing is an ongoing journey helps us stay patient with ourselves, forgiving of our perceived missteps, and hopeful for the progress we're yet to make.

Stories of Isis' Undying Perseverance

The tales of Isis offer rich insights into the nature of undying perseverance. While many know her as a goddess of magic and motherhood, her role as a beacon of resilience and relentless pursuit of healing is perhaps most inspiring.

In one of the most poignant stories, after the treachery of Set, Isis was left to mourn and find the scattered pieces of her beloved Osiris. Instead of succumbing to despair, she embarked on a quest, facing numerous challenges and obstacles. Her journey was not just to recover the pieces of Osiris, but also a deeper journey of personal healing, of dealing with loss, betrayal, and the stark pain of grief.

Her dedication wasn't driven by a desire for a final moment of resolution but by an innate understanding that every step she took was a step towards healing. The culmination wasn't just the resurrection of Osiris, but also the reclamation of her own strength, power, and purpose.

This story serves as a poignant reminder. Our healing, like Isis', is built upon layers of experiences, challenges, setbacks, and victories. Just as Isis didn't find all of Osiris' pieces in one place or at one time, our healing doesn't come all at once but in fragments, moments, and revelations spread across the expanse of our lives.

Embracing Every Phase of the Healing Path

In our journey of continuous healing, it's crucial to honor and embrace every phase we go through. The highs, the lows, the stagnation, and the progress — every part of the journey has its purpose.

The moments of stagnation, often mistaken for regression, are times of deep internal work. They are the pauses where our soul catches its breath, where our heart recalibrates, and where our spirit gathers strength for the next leap.

Similarly, the moments of pain and relapse, while challenging, are equally valuable. They remind us of the areas that need more attention, of wounds that perhaps weren't entirely healed, offering us another opportunity to address, understand, and mend them.

Even the peaks, the moments where we feel we've made significant progress, are not endpoints but mere milestones. They celebrate how far we've come, but they also gently nudge us forward, reminding us that there's more to discover, more to heal, and more to evolve into.

To embrace every phase of the healing path means to honor our journey in its entirety, without judgment. It means understanding that healing isn't linear. Like the spiral dance of the universe, it moves in cycles — sometimes taking us inward, closer to our pain, only to lead us outward into growth and transformation.

The continuous journey of healing, as portrayed through the tales and teachings of Isis, is a profound lesson in resilience, understanding, and growth. While we all have our unique paths and challenges, the core truth remains — healing is an ever-evolving dance, a river that's always flowing. By recognizing this, and by drawing inspiration from the undying perseverance of Isis, we equip ourselves to embrace, cherish, and navigate every twist and turn of our own healing journey.

Chapter 20: The Final Benediction

As we come to the close of this enlightening journey through the world of Isis, the ancient Egyptian deity of magic and healing, it's essential to take a moment to reflect on the myriad lessons and insights we've gathered. It's in such moments of introspection that we truly assimilate our learnings and decide how to integrate them into our daily lives.

The tales of Isis are not merely historical relics to be admired from a distance; they are living, breathing narratives that beckon us to understand a deeper truth about the world and our place within it. From the very outset, we set forth on a mission to uncover the essence of Isis's teachings — the heart of which is the transformative power of healing, resilience, and hope.

But what does it truly mean to heal? Healing is not merely the absence of disease or discomfort. It's the holistic understanding of one's being, the integration of the mind, body, and spirit, and the continuous endeavor to attain a state of balance. It's about acknowledging our wounds, both seen and unseen, and allowing the magic within and around us to mend those fractures.

Throughout our exploration, we encountered the maternal spirit that Isis embodies. It serves as a gentle reminder that all of us, irrespective of gender or background, harbor a nurturing energy within. It's this energy that compels us to take care of others and ourselves, to protect, to love unconditionally, and to guide those who look up to us.

This book, while firmly rooted in the past, speaks to the contemporary soul. The struggles and triumphs of Isis mirror our own battles and victories. Her resilience in the face of adversity serves as a testament to the indomitable human spirit. And so, while the goddess's stories may be ancient, their essence is timeless.

It is now time to offer our gratitude to the deity who has been our guide and mentor throughout this journey. Let us close our eyes, take a deep breath, and center ourselves, ready to connect with the divine.

A Prayer to Isis for Continuous Guidance

Oh, Isis, Great Mother, Keeper of Mysteries,

We stand before you, humbled by your wisdom and grace.

Guide us, oh benevolent deity, as we navigate the vast expanse of life,

Help us harness the power of healing, magic, and maternal love that you embody.

As the sun sets and gives way to the moonlit night,

Be our beacon, our North Star, illuminating the path ahead.

In moments of doubt, let your stories remind us of our inner strength,

In times of sorrow, let your resilience inspire hope in our hearts.

Oh, Great Isis, assist us in embracing the magical healer that resides within,

Let our actions reflect your teachings, and our spirits soar high, free from worldly chains.

As we conclude, let us internalize the essence of this prayer. The invocation is not just a plea for assistance but a recognition of our inherent capabilities. Each one of us possesses an innate magic – a force that can heal, inspire, and transform. It's a reservoir of untapped potential, waiting for the right moment to manifest.

"Embracing the Magical Healer within" is not a one-time act but a lifelong journey. It requires patience, persistence, and above all, faith – faith in the divine, faith in the teachings of Isis, and most importantly, faith in oneself.

Every time you feel lost or overwhelmed, remember the stories and lessons from this book. Let them serve as a compass, guiding you back to your center, back to the magical healer within.

May the wisdom of Isis illuminate your path, and may you find the strength to rise, heal, and thrive, no matter the challenges that lie ahead. Remember, the journey might end here, but the lessons and the magic? They are eternal.

And so, with a heart full of gratitude and a spirit brimming with hope, we bid adieu, not as an end but as a benediction — a blessing for the many adventures and discoveries that await you.

Printed in Great Britain
by Amazon

38877503R00066